Siren Salamander
What Is an Amphibian?

By LINDA AYERS

Illustrated by KATY HUDSON

Music Arranged and Produced by MARK OBLINGER

CANTATA
LEARNING

WWW.CANTATALEARNING.COM

CANTATA LEARNING

Published by Cantata Learning
1710 Roe Crest Drive
North Mankato, MN 56003
www.cantatalearning.com

A note to educators and librarians from the publisher: Cantata Learning has provided the following data to assist in book processing and suggested use of Cantata Learning product.

Publisher's Cataloging-in-Publication Data
Prepared by Librarian Consultant: Ann-Marie Begnaud
Library of Congress Control Number: 2015958173
 Siren Salamander : What Is an Amphibian?
 Series: Animal World : Animal Kingdom Boogie
 By Linda Ayers
 Illustrated by Katy Hudson
 Summary: Discover the characteristics of salamanders, frogs, and other amphibians in this fun song paired with beautiful illustrations.
 ISBN: 978-1-63290-606-9 (library binding/CD)
 ISBN: 978-1-63290-649-6 (paperback/CD)
Suggested Dewey and Subject Headings:
 Dewey: E 597.8
 LCSH Subject Headings: Amphibians – Anatomy – Juvenile literature. | Amphibians – Behavior – Juvenile literature. | Amphibians – Physiology – Juvenile literature. | Amphibians – Songs and Music – Texts. | Amphibians – Juvenile sound recordings.
 Sears Subject Headings: Amphibians. | School songbooks. | Children's songs. | World music.
 BISAC Subject Headings: JUVENILE NONFICTION / Animals / Reptiles & Amphibians. | JUVENILE NONFICTION / Music / Songbooks. | JUVENILE NONFICTION / Science & Nature / Zoology.

Book design and art direction, Tim Palin Creative
Editorial direction, Flat Sole Studio
Music direction, Elizabeth Draper
Music arranged and produced by Mark Oblinger

Printed in the United States of America in North Mankato, Minnesota.
072016   0335CGF16

What is an amphibian? Frogs, salamanders, toads, and **newts** are amphibians. They are all animals that start their lives living in the water and breathing through **gills**. As they grow, most amphibians develop lungs. But a few, such as the siren salamander, keep their gills, too.

To learn more about amphibians,
turn the page and sing along!

Siren salamander, **slimy** and brown,
sat by the water, worried he might drown.

Along came a spotty little **mudpuppy**.

She sang, "Don't worry.

You have gills to help you breathe!"

Amphibians hatch from jelly eggs.
Amphibians, as they grow,
    their bodies change.

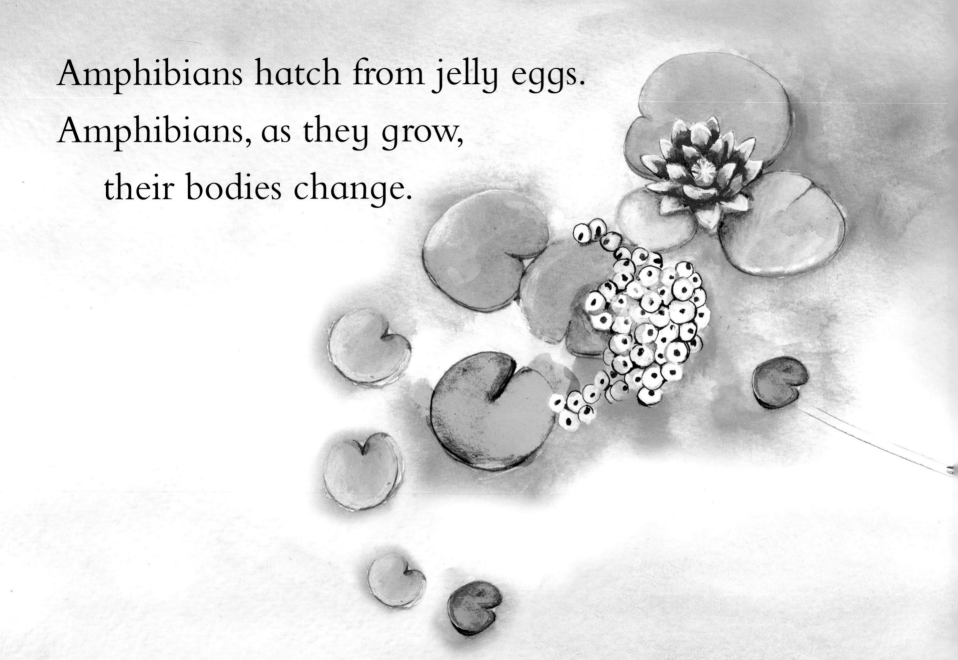

They live in the water and on land.
With smooth, slimy skin, they're amphibians.

Amphibians.
Amphibians.

Amphibians eat more than just bugs,
like snails and spiders and even slimy slugs.

They eat mice and snakes, worms and more,
and other amphibians and even birds that soar!

Amphibians hatch from jelly eggs.
Amphibians, as they grow, their bodies change.

They live in the water and on land.

With smooth, slimy skin, they're amphibians.

Amphibians.

Amphibians.

There are many kinds of amphibians,
like newts, salamanders, and **caecilians**.
So are frogs and toads, and did you know,
they all start as **tadpoles**. Just watch them grow!

Amphibians hatch from jelly eggs.

Amphibians, as they grow, their bodies change.

They live in the water and on land.
With smooth, slimy skin,
   they're amphibians.

Amphibians.
Amphibians.

Can you move like an amphibian?
Wiggle like a tadpole!

Can you move like an amphibian?
Jump like a frog!

Can you move like an amphibian?
Crawl like a salamander!

Can you move like an amphibian?
Hop, toad. Hop!

Siren salamander, slimy and brown,

sat in the water. He knew he wouldn't drown.

Along came a spotty little mudpuppy.

She sang, "It's nice we have gills to help us breathe!"

Amphibians. Yeah, amphibians.
Amphibians. Yeah, amphibians.

SONG LYRICS
Siren Salamander

Siren salamander, slimy and brown,
sat by the water, worried he might drown.
Along came a spotty little mudpuppy.
She sang, "Don't worry.
You have gills to help you breathe!"

Amphibians hatch from jelly eggs.
Amphibians, as they grow, their bodies change.

They live in the water and on land.
With smooth, slimy skin, they're amphibians.

Amphibians.
Amphibians.

Amphibians eat more than just bugs,
like snails and spiders and even slimy slugs.
They eat mice and snakes, worms and more,
and other amphibians and even birds that soar!

Amphibians hatch from jelly eggs.
Amphibians, as they grow, their bodies change.

They live in the water and on land.
With smooth, slimy skin, they're amphibians.

Amphibians.
Amphibians.

There are many kinds of amphibians,
like newts, salamanders, and caecilians.
So are frogs and toads, and did you know,
they all start as tadpoles. Just watch them grow!

Amphibians hatch from jelly eggs.
Amphibians, as they grow, their bodies change.

They live in the water and on land.
With smooth, slimy skin, they're amphibians.

Amphibians.
Amphibians.

Can you move like an amphibian?
Wiggle like a tadpole!

Can you move like an amphibian?
Jump like a frog!

Can you move like an amphibian?
Crawl like a salamander!

Can you move like an amphibian?
Hop, toad. Hop!

Siren salamander, slimy and brown,
sat in the water. He knew he wouldn't drown.
Along came a spotty little mudpuppy.
She sang, "It's nice we have gills to help us breathe!"

Amphibians. Yeah, amphibians.
Amphibians. Yeah, amphibians.

Siren Salamander

World
Mark Oblinger

Verse

1. Si-ren sal-a-man-der, slim-y and brown, sat by the wa-ter, wor-ried he might drown. A-long came a spot-ty lit-tle

mud-pup-py. She sang, "Don't wor-ry. You have gills to help you breathe!"

Chorus

Am-phib-i-ans hatch from jel-ly eggs. Am-phib-i-ans, as they grow, their bod-ies change. They live in the wa-ter

and on land. With smooth, slim-y skin, they're am-phib-i-ans. Am-phib-i-ans. Am-phib-i-ans.

Verse 2
Amphibians eat more than just bugs,
like snails and spiders and even slimy slugs.
They eat mice and snakes, worms and more,
and other amphibians and even birds that soar!

Chorus

Verse 3
There are many kinds of amphibians,
like newts, salamanders, and caecilians.
So are frogs and toads, and did you know,
they all start as tadpoles. Just watch them grow!

Chorus

Breakdown

Can you move like an am-phib-i-an? Wig-gle like a tad-pole! Can you move like an am-phib-i-an? Jump like a frog!

Can you move like an am-phib-i-an? Crawl like a sal-a-man-der! Can you move like an am-phib-i-an? Hop, toad. Hop!

Verse 4
Siren salamander, slimy and brown,
sat in the water. He knew he wouldn't drown.
Along came a spotty little mudpuppy.
She sang, "It's nice we have gills to help us breathe!"

Coda

Am-phib-i-ans. Yeah, am-phib-i-ans. Am-phib-i-ans. Yeah, am-phib-i-ans.

GLOSSARY

caecilians—wormlike amphibians

gills—body parts that fish and amphibians use to breathe underwater

mudpuppy—a type of salamander that lives its entire life in water

newts—a type of salamander with short legs and a long tail

slimy—wet and slippery to the touch

tadpoles—amphibians between the egg and adult stages of life; tadpoles live in water.

GUIDED READING ACTIVITIES

1. If you were an amphibian, would you want to spend more of your time in the water or on land? Why?

2. On page 6, the siren salamander is afraid to go swimming. Have you ever been afraid to do something fun? How did you get over that fear?

3. Frogs change a lot during their lives. Draw a picture showing the four stages of life of a frog: egg, tadpole, froglet (a small frog with a tail), and adult.

TO LEARN MORE

Carr, Aaron. *Salamander*. New York: AV2 by Weigl, 2016.

Hall, Katharine. *Amphibians and Reptiles: A Compare and Contrast Book*. Mt. Pleasant, SC: Arbordale Publishing, 2015.

Kaspar, Anna. *What's an Amphibian?* New York: PowerKids Press, 2012.

Martin, Isabel. *Amphibians: A Question and Answer Book*. North Mankato, MN: Capstone Press, 2015.